"Pidgy"

by Clare E. Rojas

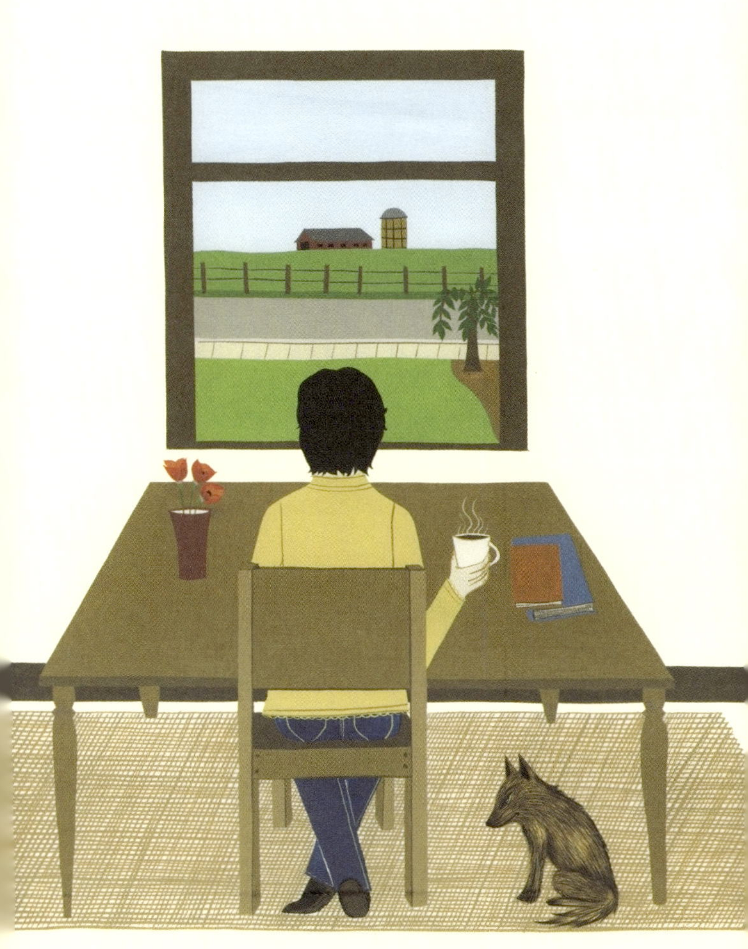

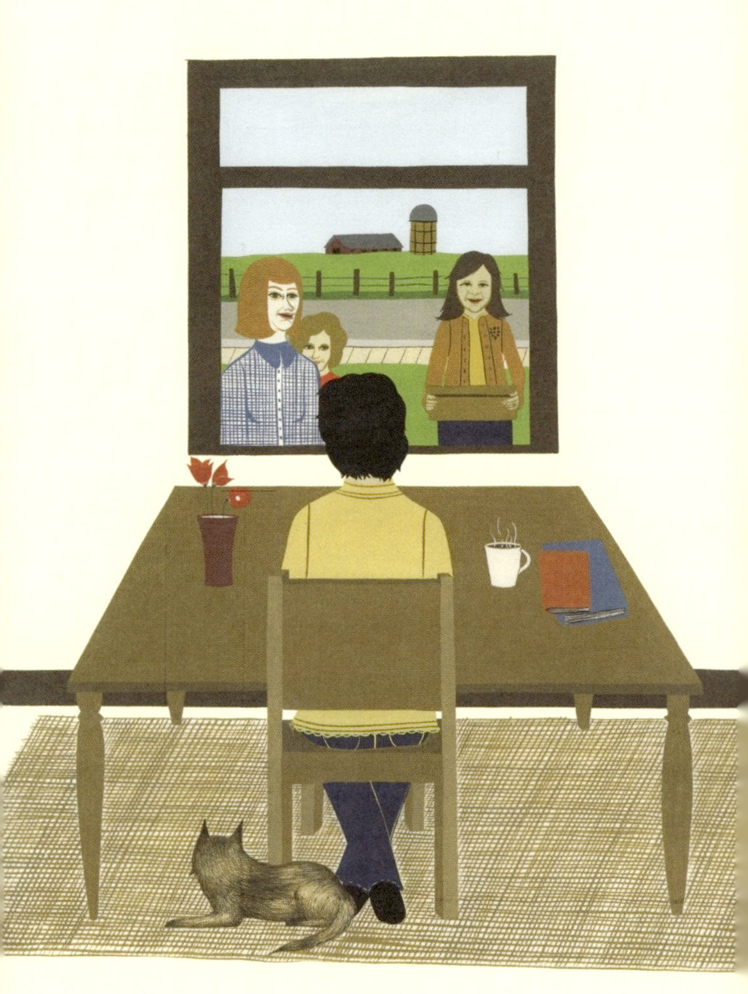

Knock, knock, knock. "Woof, woof, woof, bark." Ms. Vireo and Lucy, a brindle-mix dog, were not expecting company. Ms. Vireo put her book down and went to the door.

Three little neighborhood girls, Peddle, Eliza and Francy, stood on Ms. Vireo's porch with a wiggling shoebox in hand. "Ms. Vireo, do you by any chance know how to raise a baby bird? We found him on our doorstep and don't know how to take care of him? He survived falling out of the nest after the storm a few days ago. My Dad put him back and then he fell out again."

Ms. Vireo stood there looking at the box and the three concerned little faces. She smiled and said to the girls, "Let's walk to the corner store to get supplies. Looks like this little guy is one tough survivor. He wants to live and knew just where to go to get the help he needs." This made the three little girls feel proud and each walked with an extra little bounce in their step.

They walked a few blocks to the local market with the baby bird in the shoebox.

Ms. Vireo had Peddle get one can of dog food, Eliza got a box of baby rice cereal, the powdered kind, and Francy was to get a carton of milk.

Ms. Vireo got a roll of paper towels, a pie pan for the birdbath and a few other essential items.

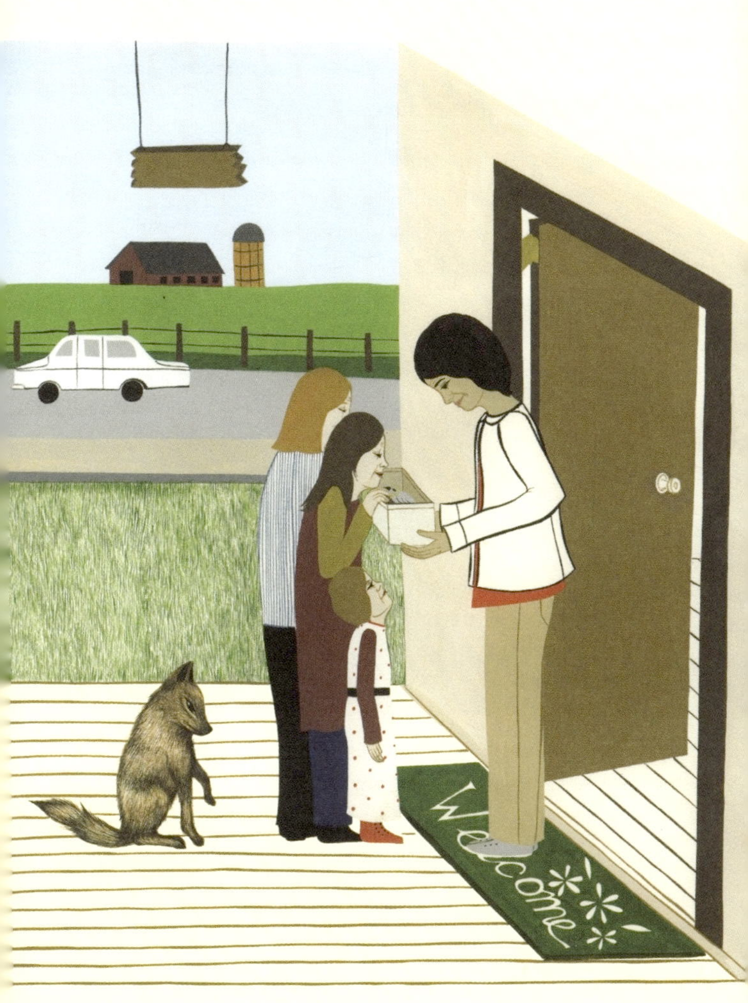
Welcome

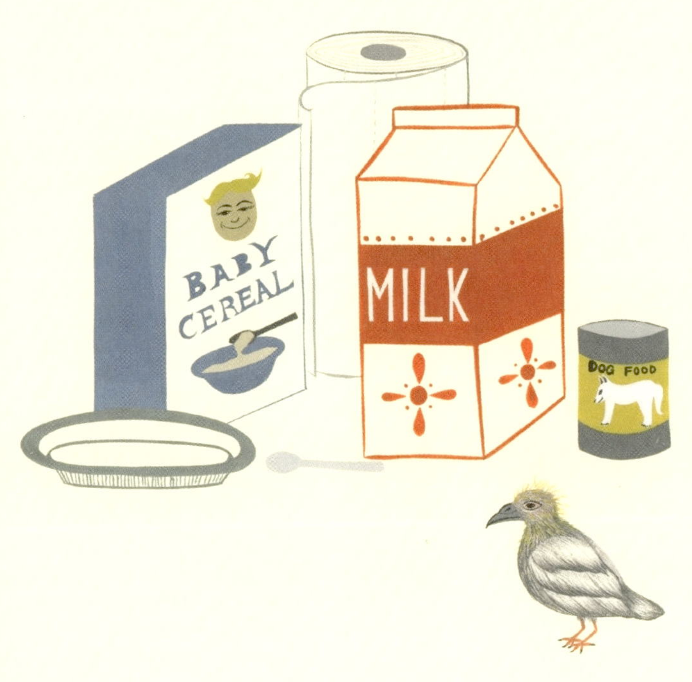
BABY
CEREAL
MILK
DOG FOOD

They walked back to Ms. Vireo's house with the supplies and very large smiles on their faces.

Ms. Vireo gave the girls a peanut butter jar and said, "Mix one spoonful of dog food, one spoonful of cereal and one spoonful of milk." Each girl put her ingredients in and Ms. Vireo shook the jar.

Francy opened the lid and immediately the baby bird began squawking and flapping his wings against his pink and grey-skinned little body.

The baby was hungry.

Ms. Vireo handed each girl an apron and said, "You will thank me for this." The girls put their aprons on and waited with anticipation.

Ms. Vireo took a spoon out of her apron and got a spoonful of goop for the baby. She placed the spoon under his beak and the bird ate every last drop while shaking his head back and forth. Food went flying everywhere!

What a cute little mess this baby was! And this is what they decided to name this precious little creature.

The girls asked Ms. Vireo if she would keep "Baby" at her house if they promised to come and help feed it every day after school.

Ms. Vireo agreed, and Peddle, Eliza, and Francy walked home for dinner.

The next day, after school, the three girls ran to Ms. Vireo's house with their aprons on and ready as they rang the doorbell.

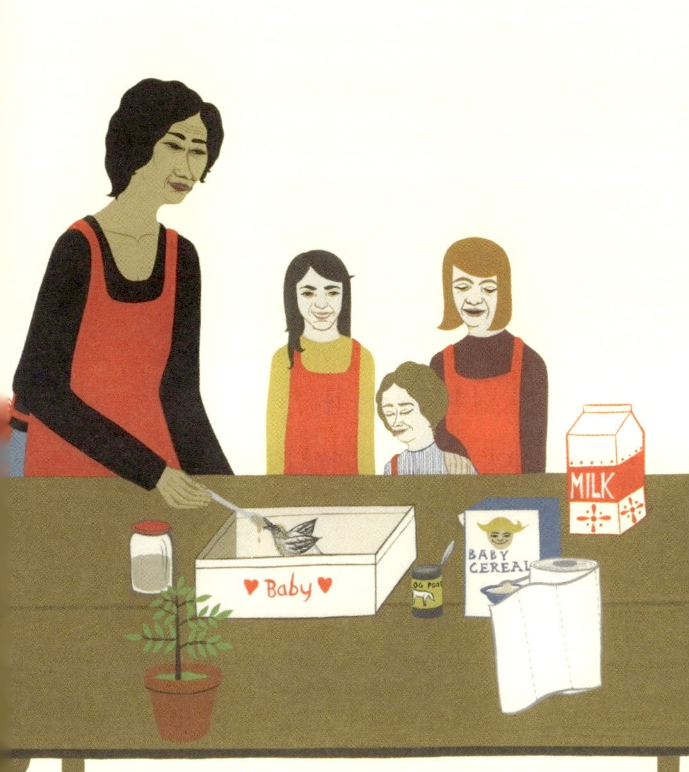
MILK
BABY
CEREAL
Baby

Ms. Vireo came to the door with Baby in her hands. The little bird was about three inches long, with hardly any feathers covering his little pinkish body. His beak was heavy-looking for the little neck that had to hold it up and his eyes were a pale grey. On the top of Baby's head were bright yellow fuzz feathers that stuck straight up and seemed to cover his little neck as well.

"Hello Girls!" Ms. Vireo said with a grin. "How was school today?" "It was great!!" Eliza said. "How is our Baby?" The little bird began tilting his head to get a better look at the girls' faces and then began gently tapping his wings against his little body in excitement. The girls decided this was the 'hungry dance'.

The three girls began doing this dance at home for their parents when they were ready to eat dinner themselves.

Ms. Vireo had all the girls sit down in her backyard watching Baby clumsily walk around, tripping over the taller pieces of grass. Ms. Vireo went inside to get some lemonade and a snack for the girls.

Lucy, Ms. Vireo's dog, was a bird dog and it took every ounce of discipline to keep her from chasing this little creature. Lucy sat on the outside of the circle and watched out of the corner of her eyes, every once in a while licking her lips and whining.

Ms. Vireo handed each girl a glass of lemonade and Baby a small plate of water. As the girls sipped the delicious sweet drink, Baby sipped the delicious water.

Next, Ms. Vireo brought out a plate of shortbread cookies and a small plate of food for Baby, and while the girls ate their cookies Ms. Vireo fed Baby. Then each girl took a turn feeding Baby. First Eliza took the spoon. She held it under the beak just like Ms. Vireo showed her, and Baby decided to fling food on his head. Then Francy took the spoon and Baby proceeded to flick food all over his body by flapping his left wing in the food, making even more of a mess.

Peddle was the last to try and thought she would outsmart Baby by placing the spoon on the ground. But, Baby outsmarted Peddle and decided to step in the food. By the time lunch was over Baby was drenched in goop.

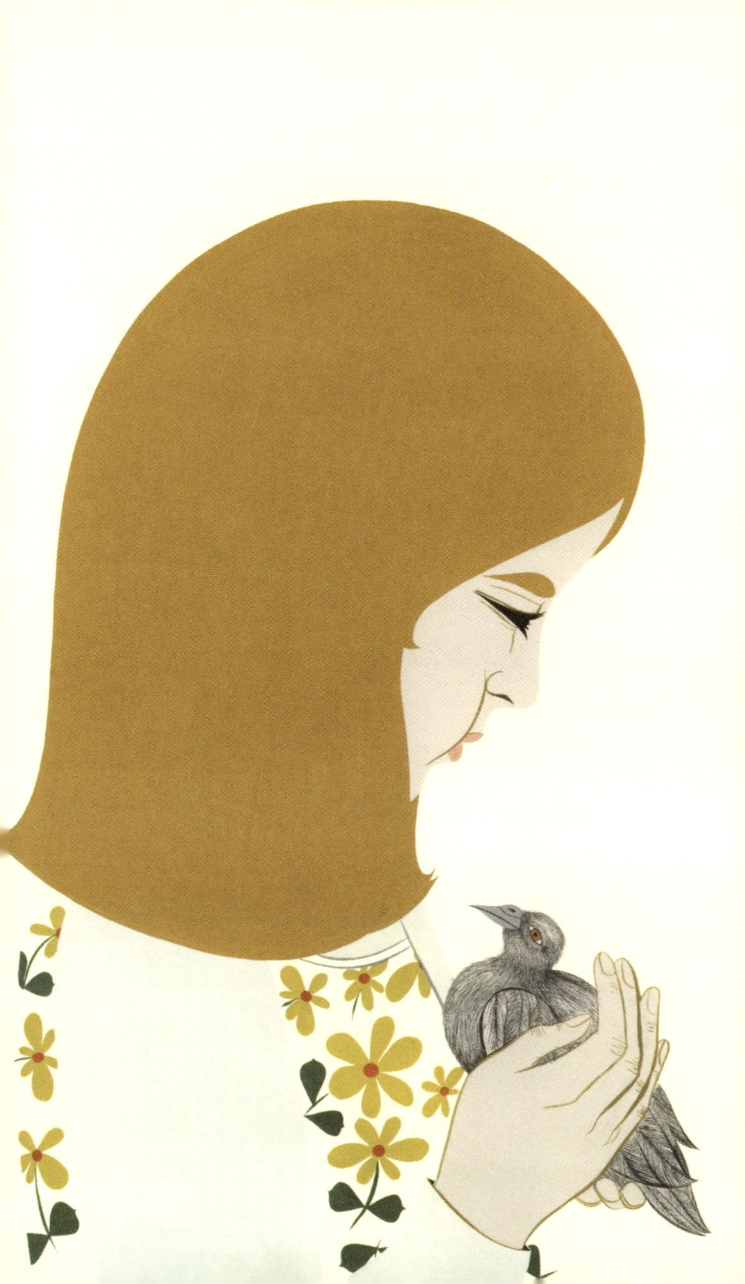

Lucy came over and sniffed the goop creature, and to everyone's surprise gently licked Baby. Ms. Vireo and the girls stood laughing at the scene taking place before their eyes. It seems Baby even won over Lucy with his comedy routine.

Ms. Vireo brought out the pie pan with a bit of warm water and placed it in the grass next to Baby. She handed each of the girls a paper towel. "It's time for Baby's bath." Ms. Vireo gently held Baby and placed him in the warm bath water. She cleaned the food that was stuck on his feet like shoes to reveal beautiful little pink feet and perfect toenails. She cleaned off his head with a towel and tried to get under Baby's wing to clean out the food that had made it in there.

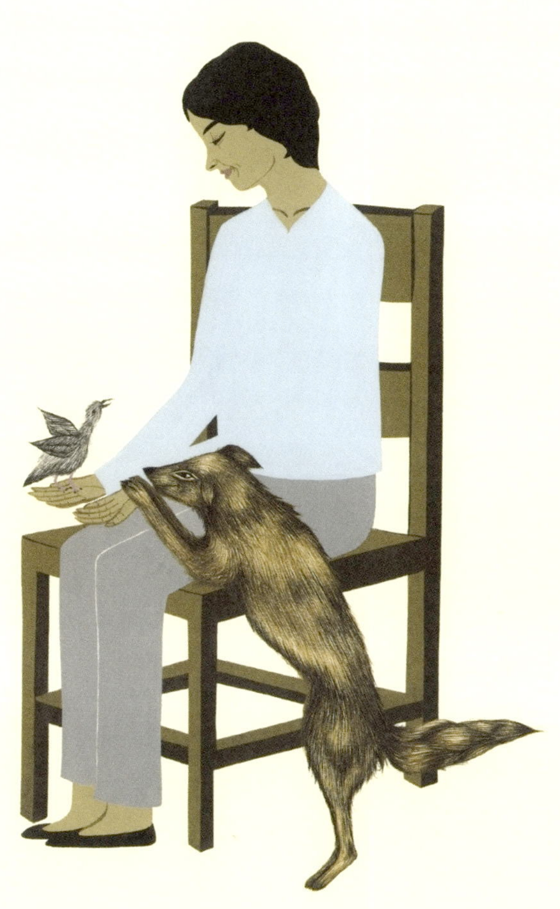

The girls each took a turn gently drying off Baby and he closed his eyes enjoying all the love he was getting. Baby walked over to where Lucy had found a patch of sunshine and sat down next to her to sleep. Lucy was happy to share her patch of sunshine with her new friend.

Francy asked Ms. Vireo if she thought Baby might be a hawk. Eliza thought maybe a falcon and Peddle thought he might be a bluebird. A hawk was majestic and a beautiful flyer, falcons were beautiful and made the coolest sound, and bluebirds, well, they were bluebirds. It constantly amazed the girls to think up what kind of powerful bird this little creature might grow into.

Ms. Vireo told the girls the best way to find out was to go spy on the nest that Baby fell out of, and that way they would be able to find the parents.

They walked down the street to the little neighborhood park where there were lots of pine, maple and oak trees. These trees were homes to all sorts of little creatures. There were squirrels, chipmunks, woodpeckers, hawks, falcons, blue jays, crows, robins and cardinals.

The trees sounded like a symphony from this band of animals just doing what they do every day.

Francy, the oldest of the three girls, remembered where the nest was, and they slowly walked over and peeked in between the branches.

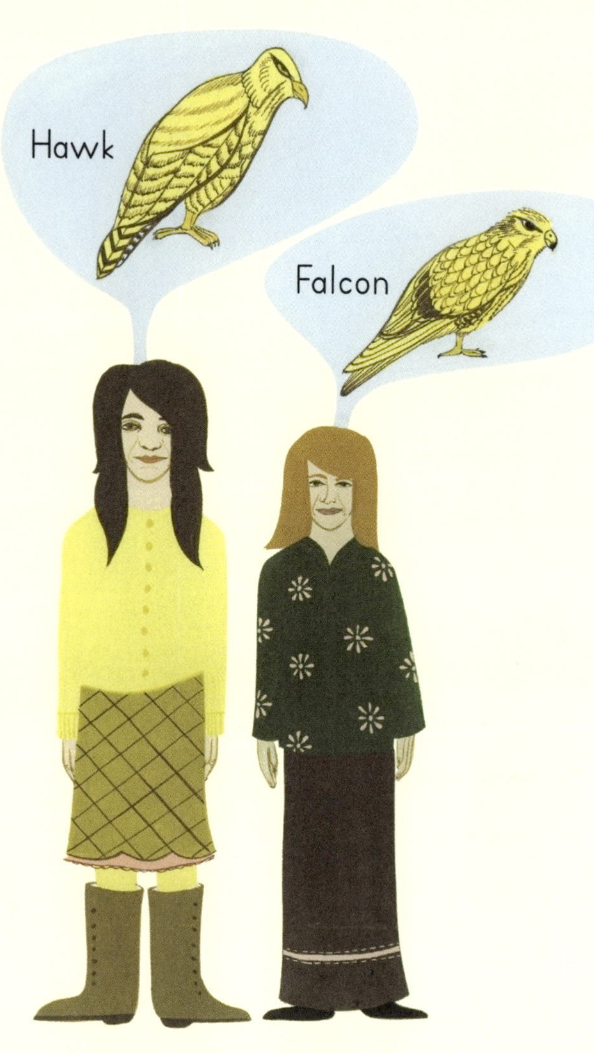
Hawk
Falcon
Francy
Eliza

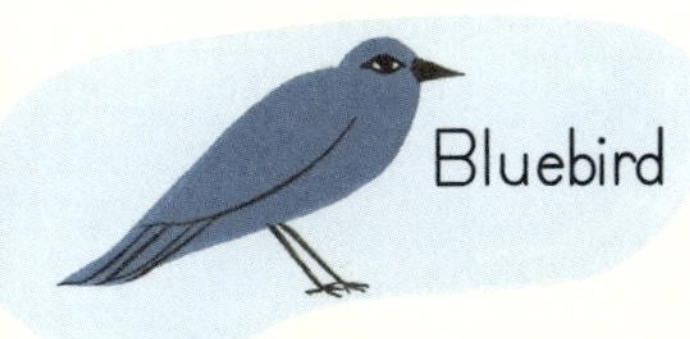

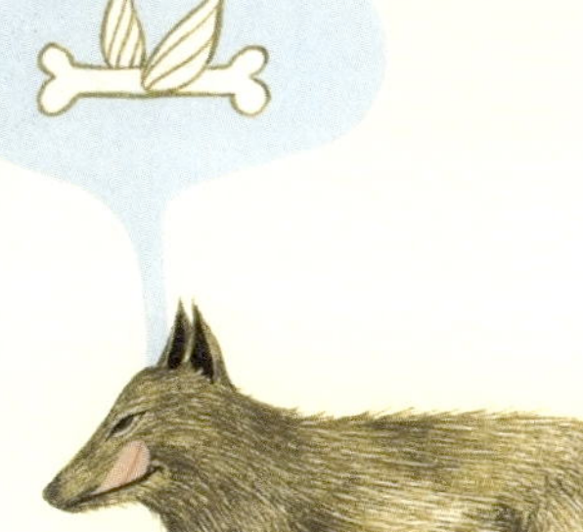

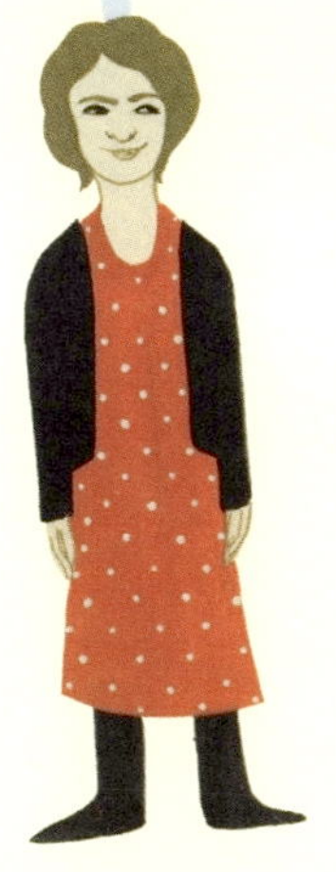

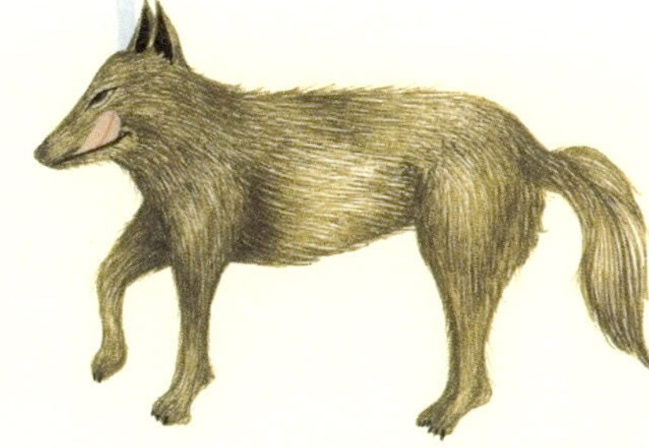

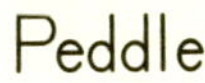

Lucy

There sat, to everyone's disbelief, a mother pigeon. Baby was a pigeon? Ms. Vireo could see this was not what the girls expected. "It's just a dirty pigeon, Ms. Vireo. That is not as exciting as a falcon," Eliza exclaimed. Peddle, all of a sudden, was more interested in her homework and started to walk home. Francy looked at the funny-looking little bird and she still loved him no matter what he was. Ms. Vireo put her arm around Eliza and Francy and called out to Peddle, "Come back here, Peddle. I have something to tell you three." Peddle turned around in disappointment and walked back.

"You know," Ms. Vireo said, "this little creature does not know he is not a falcon, a hawk, or some beautiful colored bird."

"All this little creature knows is that he is hungry; he is scared and needs our help to survive. How about we take care of him and see if we can't find out something amazing about pigeons?"

"Pidgy", as the girls had now renamed him, began to flap his wings. He liked the idea of being loved unconditionally and was probably hungry again too.

Ms. Vireo gave the girls an assignment. Tomorrow after school they were to go to the library and research pigeons, and bring some books back with them that they could read together.

The next day, after school, the three girls met at the public library and asked the librarian for some help.

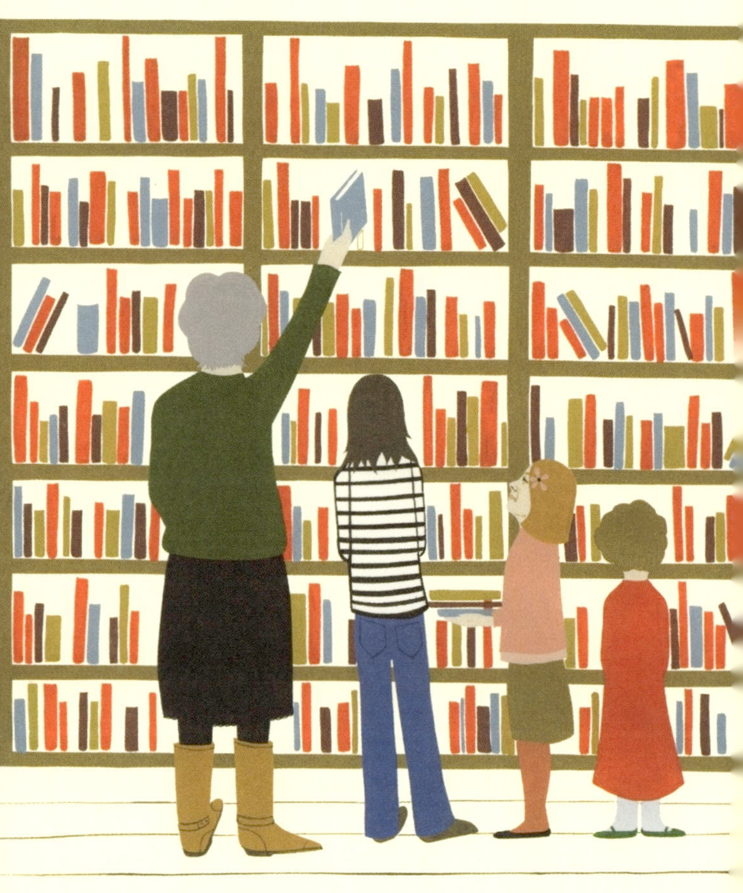

"Excuse me", Francy said. "Could you please help us? We have rescued a baby pigeon and need some information about what they like to eat and how to take care of them."

The librarian thought for a second then walked over to the animal section with the girls and began to pull out a bunch of different books. When her arms were full, she handed Francy the stack and pointed to a table, and Francy walked over to set the books down. Then Eliza came over to the table with a pile of books as well and then Peddle came with even more.

Each girl had her own stack of books all about pigeons. Each one read and read, and began to take notes on the information they were gathering.

Three hours had gone by and the girls had not even read half of the books. They decided to check the rest of the books out and take them to Ms. Vireo's house to read more about pigeons. To their surprise, pigeons were incredible birds.

The library had carts for the girls to borrow and so they rolled their books home behind them.

When they got to Ms. Vireo's house they rang the doorbell. Ms. Vireo called, "I am out back girls, with Pidgy and Lucy!"

The girls rolled the books to the backyard. They could not believe their eyes! Pidgy was sitting on Lucy's back pecking at her fur, and Lucy loved it!

"Girls, Pidgy must think he is a dog," Ms. Vireo said.

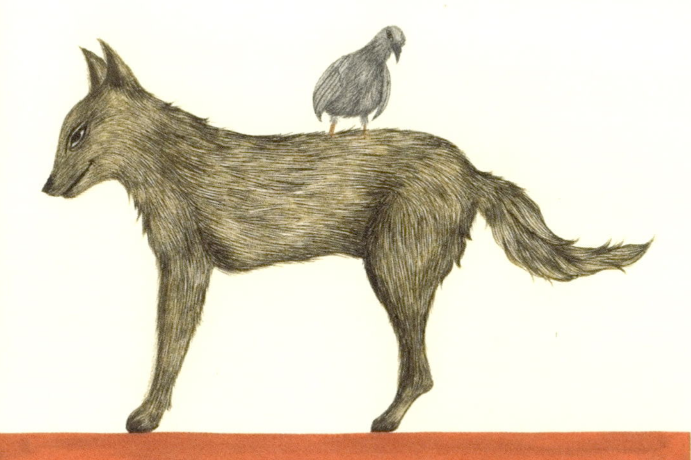

"He and Lucy have been cuddling all morning and chasing all the other birds out of the yard. Lucy even shared her bone, letting Pidgy peck at it."

The girls were so excited to share the information they gathered at the library about pigeons. "Ms. Vireo," Eliza said, as she pulled out a book and began to read from it, "did you know that Pidgy is called a domesticated rock pigeon and fossils confirm its existence for at least three hundred thousand years!!!"

Francy found out that there was an award for passenger pigeons called the Dickin Medal, instituted by Maria Dickin in 1917. She was an animal welfare pioneer from London. During World War II, thirty–two pigeons were given this medal for their bravery in saving lives.

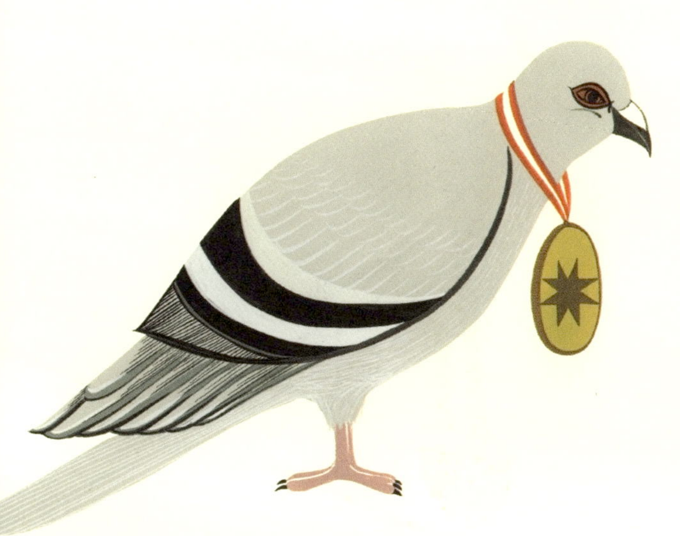

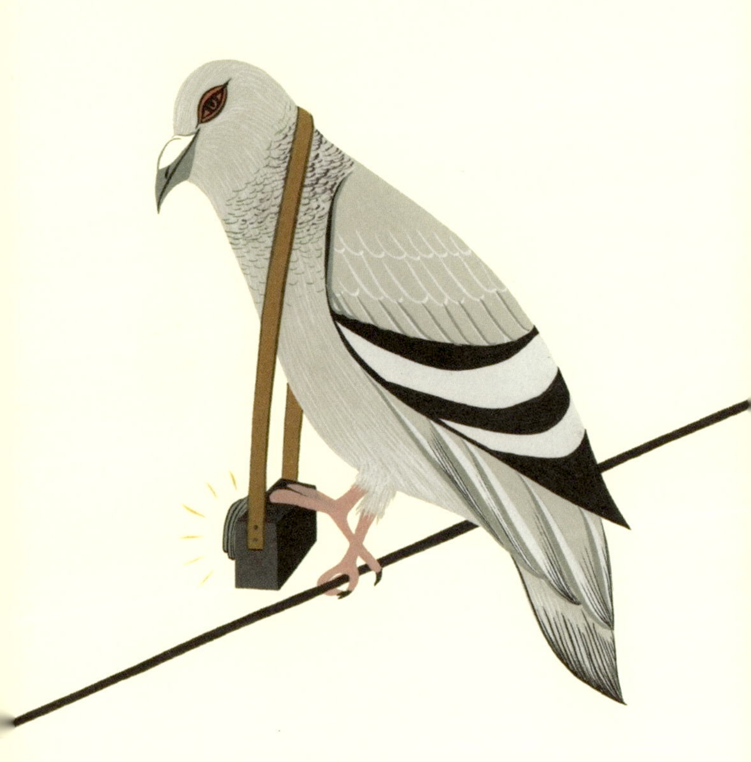

Peddle found out there was a man named Julius Neubronner who used pigeons to deliver urgent medications to hospitals around 1903. Around this time, one of the pigeons got lost in the fog and was about four weeks late, but arrived safe and sound. He was inspired by this pigeon to equip his pigeons with cameras.

The girls laughed at the thought of pigeons holding cameras.

New grown-up feathers began to replace Pidgy's pale yellow feathers and they began to make a pattern of grey and light grey.

The tail feathers began to grow large and Pidgy loved to stretch them out. It was so cute to see his little feet curl up and out as they stretched.

His wings began to grow strong and Pidgy would stretch them out high in the air when it was hot outside and he needed to cool down.

The three girls and Ms. Vireo began to teach Pidgy how to fly by gently holding him at about waist height and letting him go. And slowly they would raise Pidgy higher and higher, and eventually he could glide down to the ground as graceful as any hawk or eagle.

Pidgy practiced flying by chasing Lucy around the yard. Ms. Vireo would spy on the two friends. It was so sweet to see how close they had become.

Teaching Pidgy how to fly up compared to down was more difficult.

But Pidgy figured it out and loved to perch on the light above the back door or in his favorite plum tree. As Pidgy's flying grew stronger, he began exploring outside of the yard and around the neighborhood. Sometimes when Ms. Vireo got home from work and did not see Pidgy in the tree or on the light, she would call to Pidgy. Soon, from a distant rooftop or telephone wire, Pidgy would come and land on Ms. Vireo's head. She was so proud of how well Pidgy was growing up.

Pidgy began to grow iridescent feathers on his neck that reflected light like a rainbow. This was the tell-tale sign that Pidgy was a boy. The lady pigeons had longer more elegant necks, but were less iridescent.

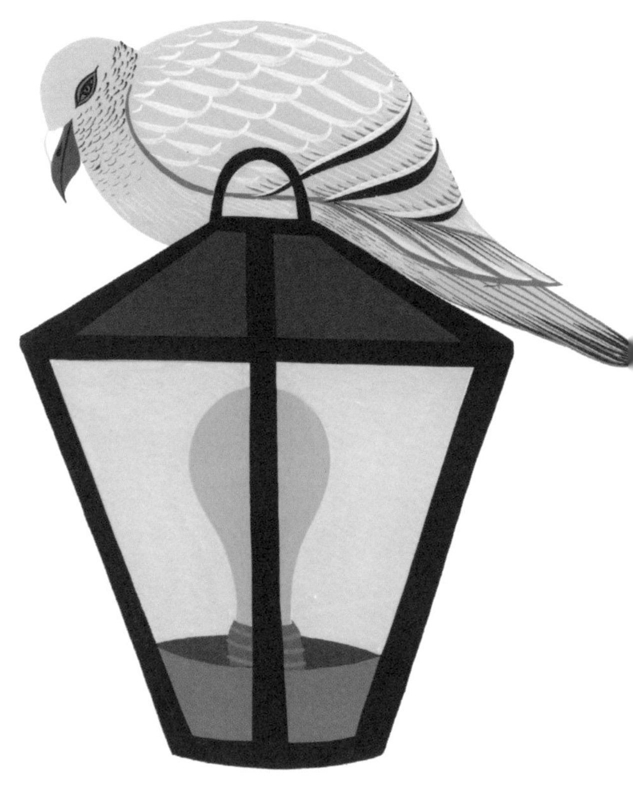

Pidgy was old enough now to eat raw uncooked rice, and so the girls and Ms. Vireo would leave rice and water out for Pidgy at each of their houses. Pidgy would come and go as he pleased, visiting each of his friends. This went on for weeks.

Every evening when Pidgy was ready to go to bed he would perch on his lamppost, and Ms. Vireo would turn the light on to keep Pidgy nice and warm through the chilly nights.

One night Ms. Vireo got her nightgown on, brushed her teeth, flossed, put on her pink slippers and went to wish Pidgy a good night, and for the first time he was not there waiting. She called to him but there was no answer. A few days later she called the girls to her house.

"Girls," she said, "Pidgy must be old enough now to find a partner, a lovely lady pigeon to start a little family with. I knew when this day came we would probably no longer see Pidgy. Pidgy has not been home for a few days now and I believe this is what has happened.

You three girls should feel very proud of yourselves. We all worked together and successfully rescued and raised such an amazing sweet little bird. What a gift he has been for us."

Ms. Vireo flung her door open and ran outside like a kid, when she saw the three girls walking home from school a few weeks later. Lucy was by her side and had a HUGE doggy smile on her face.

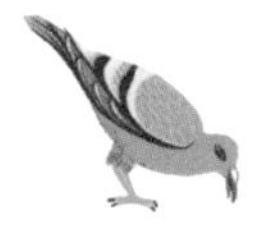

"Girls!!! Girls!!! I have to show you all something very exciting!

Come here very quietly ..."

The girls followed Ms. Vireo to the backyard where Pidgy sat perched with a lady pigeon, both on a little nest, with two eggs. Pidgy flew on Eliza's head and everyone began to laugh.

Pidgy was going to be a Dad, and a very good Dad. Every summer they enjoyed watching baby pigeons. And from that day forward, even into adulthood, every pigeon the girls saw could have been Pidgy's and received the same love and respect they gave Pidgy. Even Lucy would chase all the other birds, except for the pigeons, out of her yard for many years to come.

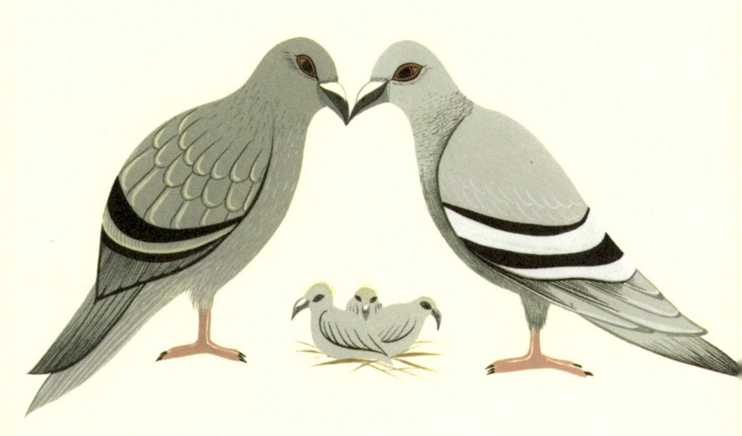

Published to accompany the exhibition
We They, We They by Clare E. Rojas

Ikon Gallery, Birmingham, UK
2 February to 21 March 2010
Curated by Nigel Prince
Assisted by Alex Lockett

The Museum of Craft and Folk Art,
San Francisco, USA
13 May to 8 August 2010
Curated by Natasha Boas

This book is dedicated to "Pidgy"

The artist would like to thank
Judy S. Rojas, Barry, Asha and Maddy,
the MOCFA and all at Ikon

MOCFA thanks Gallery Paule Anglim
for support with this publication

Edited by Nigel Prince and Judy S. Rojas
Designed by James Langdon
Printed by Veenman Drukkers
Images courtesy of the artist and
Paule Anglim, San Francisco and
Kavi Gupta, Chicago

Ikon Gallery
1 Oozells Square, Brindleyplace
Birmingham B1 2HS
T: +44 (0) 121 248 0708
F: +44 (0) 121 248 0709
www.ikon-gallery.co.uk
Registered charity no. 528892

Museum of Craft and Folk Art
51 Yerba Buena Lane, San Francisco
CA 94103
T: +1 415 227 4888
F: +1 415 227 4351
www.mocfa.org

ISBN 978 1 904864 57 8

Distributed by Cornerhouse
70 Oxford Street, Manchester M1 5NH
www.cornerhouse.org/books
T: +44 (0)161 200 1503
F: +44 (0)161 200 1504

Ikon gratefully acknowledges financial assistance from Arts Council England and Birmingham City Council

The Museum of Craft and Folk Art is generously supported by the Compton Foundation, Grants for the Arts/San Francisco Hotel Tax Fund, Walter & Elise Haas Fund, The Kimball Foundation, Harold and Gertrud Parker, The San Francisco Foundation, The Sato Foundation, Museum members, and friends

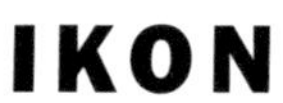

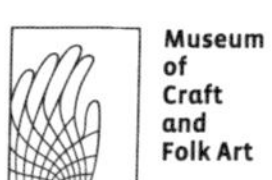

Museum
of
Craft
and
Folk Art

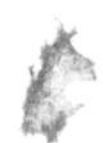